# FasTrack Export Step-by-Step Process

## Phase 3
## Build Export Market Expansion Plans

### With 23 Process Worksheets

**W Gary Winget & Sandra L Renner**

FasTrack
**GLOBALIZER®**
BUSINESS EXPANSION SYSTEM™

**FasTrack Global Expansion Solutions Inc.**
420 Summit Avenue, Suite 401
St. Paul, Minnesota 55102 • USA
Tel +1-651-222-4206 • Fax +1-651-222-5263
Info@FasTrackGlobalizer.com • www.FasTrackGlobalizer.com

This publication is one in a series titled FasTrack Export Step-by-Step Process. FasTrack and FasTrack Globalizer are registered trademarks of Global Resource Associates Inc.

Library of Congress Control Number: 2020922370

ISBN-13: 978-1-7331474-6-0

10 9 8 7 6 5 4

# TABLE OF CONTENTS

Preface                                                                5

3. Build Export Market Expansion Plans                                 9

   A.  Determine Market Entry Methods                    12

   B.  Select Market Segments & Distribution Channels     21

   C.  Determine Product, Price & Promotion               33

   D.  Develop Target Market Profiles                     50

   E.  Finalize Targeted Export Market Plans               53

   F.  Evaluate Export Market Expansion Plan Results       58

Appendices                                                             61

   A.  Feedback                                           61

   B.  FasTrack Globalizer Cloud-Based Web Solution       61

   C.  Links                                              61

# PREFACE

## FastTrack Process

The *FasTrack Export Step-by-Step Process* series was developed to assist companies, like yours, make more money by making exporting and global expansion easier.

The process will help your company not only survive but also thrive in the global market while avoiding the pain and risks frequently associated with global markets.

The *ultimate goal* of the FasTrack Process and this series is to provide a business solution that will maximize your company's success in global markets by streamlining its global expansion process and exponentially growing its sales and profits while reducing overall costs.

The FasTrack Process provides a dynamic approach to export market entry, expansion, and penetration and to globalizing your company. It follows the natural flow of the export process. It is based on the real-life experiences of the authors and of companies such as yours. It presents a step-by-step approach to quickly and successfully enter and expand into high-potential country markets and proceed to penetration and maximization of sales and profits in those markets.

Companies that succeed and profit in the global market tend to have three common characteristics that are incorporated into the FasTrack Process:

❑ *Process*

A comprehensive, boardroom-to-production floor process for planning and implementing the export process. The FasTrack process provides a highly productive, repeatable set of solutions that swiftly guides the company through the sometimes-complex maze of global growth challenges and unknowns.

❑ *Tools*

A start-to-finish, structured set of tools to address each task in the export process. The FasTrack process provides a consistent, systematic approach to each task that can be repeated and improved upon year after year.

❑ *Network*

A synergistic export planning and implementation network of export promotion organizations, export service organizations, and other outside resources. Given that every company has, to some extent, a limited set of resources and expertise to devote to exporting, the FasTrack process effectively combines a company's limited resources and expertise with those of other organizations.

**Companies are leaving hundreds of thousands, even millions, of dollars of additional sales on the table because of inefficient and ineffective global growth implementation.**

The FasTrack Process provides a solution to this problem. It is a proven, nationally recognized process. The authors were presented with the U.S. Presidential 'E' Award by the U.S. Department of Commerce for their outstanding contribution to the export expansion program of the nation.


## FasTrack Process Phases

The FasTrack Export Step-by-Step Process is available in a series of eight phases. Each phase in the series addresses one of the following phases in the FasTrack Process.

While your company may benefit by starting with the implementation of the Phase 1 process and proceeding in order to the final Phase 8 process, you may start with any phase in the FasTrack Process series based on your company's priorities and needs. However, there will be links between phases and within a phase, and you will be most successful if you follow the flow of the start-to-finish, step-by-step process in implementing the phases, modules and steps.

❑ *Phase 1. Starting Up a Successful Export Market Expansion Program*

This Phase will define the FasTrack Process, explain the differences between a global and a globalized company, and provide guidance in organizing or reorganizing your company's market expansion program. You will benchmark your company against a series of best-practice standards and define the expected outcomes of your successful export market expansion program.

❑ *Phase 2. Target High-Potential Export Markets*

You will select the company's highest potential export products and develop a synergistic export promotion organization and resource network. The major task in this phase will be identifying, selecting, and prioritizing the company's highest potential target markets.

❑ *Phase 3. Build Export Market Expansion Plans*

You will determine the most appropriate market entry method for each target market, select the customer segments to be served in each market, determine the distribution channels to be used in each market, and determine the positioning of the products that will be offered in the markets. Export plans will be finalized for each targeted market and the rest-of-world market.

❑ *Phase 4. Build a Highly Effective Export Organization*

You will start by defining the companywide export implementation processes and policies, building the companywide export teams and expertise, and selecting outside export service organizations. Your team will initiate the process of obtaining the required approvals and certifications for the target markets, internationalizing the company's materials and communications, planning participation in export promotion events, developing first-contact promotional methods and materials, and developing effective responses to buyer inquiries.

❑ *Phase 5. Build a Successful Export Distribution Network*

The tasks in this phase will provide guidance in identifying, screening, and qualifying potential distribution partners. The result will be the selection of the company's preferred partners in each target market and the negotiation of mutually beneficial agreements with each distribution partner.

❑ *Phase 6. Build Profitable Global Export Sales*

This phase will provide guidance in initiating export sales activities, responding to sales inquiries, finalizing export sales, preparing export order shipments, and shipping the orders.

❑ *Phase 7. Maximize Sales Potential Through Market Penetration*

This phase will assist in moving your company toward market penetration in its most successful export markets. You will fine-tune your operations in these markets and implement custom market penetration activities.

❑ *Phase 8. Globalize the Company's Strategy & Strategic Profile*

This phase will assess the globalization forces in your industry and transform the company's key global strategies and strategic profile.

# 3. BUILD EXPORT MARKET EXPANSION PLANS

| Phase/Modules | Start | End | Summary |
|---|---|---|---|
| BUILD EXPORT MARKET EXPANSION PLANS | | | |
| A. Determine Market Entry Methods | | | Review market entry methods, assess options, and select appropriate methods for each market. |
| B. Select Market Segments & Distribution Channels | | | Research target markets to identify segments and channels. Select segments to be served and channels to be used. Develop profiles of preferred distribution partners. |
| C. Determine Product, Price & Promotion | | | Research target markets to identify competitors, segments served, channels used, prices, terms and promotions. Analyze payment and terms options. Develop competitive price and promotions to be offered in each market. |
| D. Develop Target Market Profiles | | | State target market indicators and findings, market segments and channels, and competitors' prices and promotions. |
| E. Finalize Export Market Plans | | | Define current activities. Summarize findings and assumptions. Establish objectives and strategies. Finalize plans. Forecast sales and expenses. |
| F. Evaluate Export Market Expansion Plan Results | | | Evaluate plans and achievements. |
| EXPORT MARKET EXPANSION PLANS BUILT | | | |

# Objective

To build the company's targeted export market expansion plans for the target markets and the ROW market.

# Discussion

In the third phase of the FasTrack Process, you will build your company's targeted export market expansion plans — market segments, distribution channels, objectives, strategies, and budget.

In the first few years in which you develop an export plan, the inputs may be tentative and incomplete. However, as you progress through future annual export planning cycles, you will develop increasingly better quantitative and qualitative inputs into your decision-making process and, thus, increasingly effective export plans.

The development of the export plan is a companywide process. Approach the development of your export plan with the support and input of all the units in the company that relate to the start-to-finish export process.

# Modules

### A. Determine Market Entry Methods

Review market entry method options. Assess options in relation to target and ROW markets. Select the most appropriate market entry methods for each market.

### B. Select Market Segments & Distribution Channels

Research target markets to identify potential market segments and channels of distribution. Analyze segments and channels. Determine the appropriate channels of distribution for each market. Match potential segments and channels. Select priority market segments to be served and channels of distribution to be used. Develop profiles of preferred partners by distribution channel.

### C. Determine Product, Price & Promotion

Research target market to identify competitors. Analyze competitors' products, market segments served, channels of distribution, trade and payment terms, prices, and promotions. Analyze price and terms options. Develop competitive position in relation to product, price and promotions.

### D. Develop Target Market Profiles

State target market indicators and findings, market segments and channels of distribution, and competitors' products, prices, and promotions to be offered in each market.

### E. Finalize Export Market Plans

Define current activities. Summarize findings and assumptions. Establish objectives and strategies. Forecast sales and expenses for each market.

## F. *Evaluate Export Market Plan Results*

Review the sales and other objectives for the target and ROW markets. Determine the degree to which each objective was achieved. Develop adjustments in the export plan.

## Definitions

"Export Plan" refers to a near-term (e.g., one year), specific-thinking process that defines the products, markets, market segments, channels of distribution, objectives, strategies, and resources allocated by the company to export markets. The export plan should be consistent with and support the companywide annual and strategic plans.

# 3A. Determine Market Entry Methods

| Module/Steps | Start | End | Worksheets |
|---|---|---|---|
| DETERMINE MARKET ENTRY METHODS | | | |
| 1. Assess Market Entry Methods | | | Market Entry Method Assessment |
| 2. Compare Direct/Indirect Export Methods | | | Direct/Indirect Export Market Entry Method Comparison |
| 3. Select Preferred Market Entry Methods | | | Markets & Entry Methods |
| 4. Indirect Market Entry Considerations | | | Export Intermediary Screen |
| MARKET ENTRY METHODS DETERMINED | | | |

## Objective

To determine the most appropriate market entry method for each target and ROW market.

## Discussion

There are two general approaches for entering export markets.

- Direct Export
- Indirect Export

Many times new-to-export companies will select an indirect export method because it is an "easy" way to enter export markets. However, the easy method can end up costing a company future sales and profits. If the company later decides to become a direct exporter but has given away its rights to specific high-potential markets, or even worldwide markets, it may have also given away the potential for maximizing its sales and profits in those markets.

## Steps

### 1. Assess Direct Market Entry Methods

There are six common direct market entry methods.

- *Export*
- *License*
- *Franchise*
- *Joint Venture*
- *Foreign Manufacturing*
- *Contract Manufacturing*

A company might select the export market entry method because it is generally less complex and is a lower risk method of market entry when compared to other options. However, when a company is established in a market and is moving toward the Market Penetration phase of development in a market, other options (e.g., joint venture) may become more appropriate and profitable. You may use the *Market Entry Method Assessment* worksheet (3A1) to review and assess the various options.

> **CASE EXAMPLE**. *This manufacturer of high-quality trash receptacles got into exporting because it was receiving foreign inquiries. Rather than develop the in-house expertise needed to sell their product abroad, the company worked with an Export Trading Company to handle its exports. The trading company took title to the shipment, accepted the credit risk, and handled the shipping and export paperwork. Having established that there is a significant export market for their product, the company then wanted to more aggressively market its product abroad and began a mix of export market entry options.*

### 2. Comparing Direct & Indirect Export Methods

The following discussion will help your company compare the advantages and disadvantages of the direct and indirect export market entry methods.

❑ *Direct Export*

The direct export entry method implies that your company will sell its product directly into foreign markets, usually through your own sales operation or through an agent (sometimes referred to as a manufacturer's representative) or distributor. You will be the exporter, control the introduction of your product into the export market, and, if you use your own sales operations, control the channel of distribution right to the customer or consumer.

❑ *Indirect Export*

The indirect export entry method involves the use of domestic-based export intermediaries that provide your company with an alternative to direct exporting. These companies are commonly either Export Trading Companies (ETC) or export merchants. The ETC is an independent company that buys and takes title to your product, exports it to the foreign market, and controls the introduction of your product into the market. Frequently, the company will resell the product under its own name. Your sale is a domestic sale.

> *Case Example. An exporter of Midwest dairy cattle, the company was an intermediary between foreign buyers and U.S. cattle raisers. Because of the company, hundreds of dairy producers were able to export to foreign markets. The business was successful because of the unique nature of the dairy industry and the high level of trust and expertise the company had developed with both its buyers and sellers. Producers were scattered and have limited number of cattle to sell. However, the buyer wanted a large number of animals. The company linked the needs of sellers and buyers, and made the export of cattle possible.*

❑ *Variation on Direct and Indirect Export*

There are also variations on the direct and indirect export methods described above that provide a middle ground between the direct and indirect method of market entry.

- *Export Management Company (EMC).* This is considered a direct method option that engages a domestic company to act as your company's sales agent in foreign markets – it might be thought of as an independent sales department. The EMC establishes a presence in foreign markets and solicits orders in your company's name, and your company is considered the exporter of record.

- *Consolidation Buyer.* This is an indirect export method and typically involves a foreign buyer that established a presence in your domestic market and buys and takes title to the product from several domestic suppliers. The buyer consolidates the various products into a single shipment and exports the products. In these cases, you may or may not be the exporter of record, depending on how the transaction is structured.

To assess the typical advantages and disadvantages of the direct and indirect export methods, use the *Direct/Indirect Export Market Entry Method Comparison* worksheet (3A2). There are many factors to be considered, and the worksheet helps you sort out the advantages and disadvantages of each method based on your product and organization and the target and ROW markets you are considering. You might, for example, use the direct export method for your target markets and the indirect export method for specific ROW markets.

1. **Select Preferred Market Entry Method**

Weigh the options, determine the net advantage/disadvantage for each method, and select your company's preferred market entry method for each target and ROW market. Use the *Markets & Entry Methods* worksheet (3A3) to finalize your decisions and rationale.

2. **Indirect Market Entry Considerations**

If you decide to use either the indirect export market entry method or one of the variations described above, you will have to find and select an Export Trading Company, export merchant or Export Management Company.

Ideally, you will interview several companies and assess their qualifications to sell your product in your target or ROW markets. How does the company handle its current product lines, and how satisfied are its current suppliers? Does the company have the capacity to introduce and promote your product in the target market and elsewhere? Will you offer the company an exclusive or non-exclusive right to a limited or worldwide market and for how long? Will you establish minimum performance objectives? You may use the *Export Intermediary Screen* worksheet (3A4) to interview and evaluate potential indirect export intermediaries.

You will want to consider that if you initiate an agreement with an export intermediary, this can be a potential hazard zone – you may be ceding the ability to later export directly to the defined market. Select your export intermediary carefully and negotiate an agreement with performance standards that gives you the flexibility to make future adjustments.

**Worksheet 3A1**

**MARKET ENTRY METHOD ASSESSMENT**

Purpose: To assess the market entry methods for target export and ROW markets. Directions: List target export markets and ROW market. Note advantages and disadvantages of each market entry method for each market.

Company Name/Division:             Project:        ☐ Initial ☐ Update
☐ ROW  ☐ Target Country:

| Export | License | Franchise | Joint Venture | Foreign Mfg. | Contract Mfg. | Other |
|--------|---------|-----------|---------------|--------------|---------------|-------|
|        |         |           |               |              |               |       |
|        |         |           |               |              |               |       |
|        |         |           |               |              |               |       |
|        |         |           |               |              |               |       |
|        |         |           |               |              |               |       |
|        |         |           |               |              |               |       |
|        |         |           |               |              |               |       |
|        |         |           |               |              |               |       |
|        |         |           |               |              |               |       |
|        |         |           |               |              |               |       |

Completed by:                       Date:

## Worksheet 3A2
## DIRECT/INDIRECT EXPORT MARKET ENTRY METHOD COMPARISON

Purpose: To compare the direct and indirect export market entry methods. Directions: (1) Prepare a worksheet for each prioritized Target Market (2C7) and the ROW market. (2) For the two market entry methods, evaluate advantages and disadvantages and enter a score on a scale of 0 to +10 for each advantage and a scale of -10 to 0 for each disadvantage. (3) Total the scores and number of items scored for each column; add the advantage and disadvantage scores and the number of items scored in the Total Score column; determine the Net Advantage/Disadvantage by dividing the total score by the total number of items scored.

Company Name/Division:                    Project:                         ☐Initial ☐Update

☐ROW ☐Target Market:

| Mkt Entry Method | Advantages 0=None. +10=Significant Advantage. | Score | Disadvantages -10=Significant Disadvantage. 0=None. | Score | Total Score |
|---|---|---|---|---|---|
| Direct | Develop market knowledge in-house. Develop customer knowledge in-house. Gain export experience/expertise in-house. Control distribution channels, promotion, after-sale service, quality. Control the priority given to exporting product. Profit margins could be higher. Price to customer/consumer could be lower. Other: | | Must train/hire staff. Must pay sales costs. Must learn export documentation/shipping. Export sales could be slower to develop. May compete with domestic sales resources. Management commitment required. Financial risk of collection of foreign sales. Other: | | |
| | Score Sum | + | Score Sum | - | = |
| | Number of Items Scored | = | Number of Items Scored | = | = |
| Net Advantage/Disadvantage of Direct Entry Method = (Total Score)/(Total Number of Items Scored)= | | | | | = |
| Indirect | No staff to train/hire. Need not learn export documentation/shipping. Export sales could develop more quickly. No competition with domestic sales resources. Management's commitment is not required. No financial risk other than those of a domestic sale. Other: | | Lost sales because foreign customer wants to buy directly from manufacturer. Develop no in-house knowledge of markets. Develop no in-house knowledge of customers. Gain no experience/expertise in exporting. Loss of control over distribution channels, promotion, after-sale service, quality. No control over priority given to exporting product and/or conflict of interest. Profit margins could be lower. Price could be higher for the end customer. Other: | | |
| | Score Sum | + | Score Sum | - | |
| | Number of Items Scored | = | Number of Items Scored | = | = |
| Net Advantage/Disadvantage of Indirect Entry Method (+/-Total Score)/(Total Number of Items Scored)= | | | | | = |

Comments:

Completed by:                                        Date:

# Worksheet 3A3

## MARKETS & ENTRY METHODS

Purpose: To select the specific market entry method that will be used for target and ROW markets. Directions: List Target or ROW market. Note the market entry method selected for each market and the rationale for that selection.

Company Name/Division:            Project:       ☐ Initial ☐ Update

☐ ROW ☐ Target Country:

| Market Entry Method | Rationale for Method Selected |
|---|---|
|  |  |
|  |  |
|  |  |
|  |  |
|  |  |
|  |  |
|  |  |
|  |  |
|  |  |
|  |  |
|  |  |
|  |  |

Completed by:              Date:

**Worksheet 3A4**

**EXPORT INTERMEDIARY SCREEN**

Company Name:

  Address:

  City/Postal Code/StPr/Country:

  Telephone:                Fax:                Email:

Facility Is: ☐Headquarters ☐Office ☐ Manufacturing Site ☐Warehouse ☐Research Center ☐Service Center ☐Other

Principal Officers/Owners
| | | | |
|---|---|---|---|
| Name: | Title: | Phone: | Email: |
| Name: | Title: | Phone: | Email: |
| Name: | Title: | Phone: | Email: |

Company Contacts:
| | | |
|---|---|---|
| Chief Executive: | Title: | Languages: |
| Sales Manager: | Title: | Languages: |
| Service Manager: | Title: | Languages: |
| Other: | Title: | Languages: |

Company Background:

  Year Founded:     Number Employees:     Type Ownership: ☐Corporation ☐Partnership ☐Proprietorship ☐Other

  Parent Company:

  Subsidiary Names:

  Business Activity: ☐Export Trading Company ☐Export Merchant ☐Export Management Company

    ☐Trading Company ☐Purchasing Agent ☐Broker ☐ Manufacturer/Producer ☐Other:

  Describe Business Activity:

  List Primary Products Represented:

  Annual Sales ☐USD ☐CD ☐Other:     Range: ☐<500,000 ☐<5million ☐<50million ☐ >50million

Company Interests:

  Why do you want to handle our products?

  Will you purchase our product? ☐Yes ☐No. If no, please explain:

  In which of our products are you interested?

  What quantities and when needed?

  Will you handle our product in our target market? ☐ Yes ☐ No.

   In what other territories are you interested in handling our product?

  Why do you think our product will sell in our target market and in your territory?

---

Export Intermediary Profile             Continued             Page1 of 1 of 2

Company Facilities in Market Area: ☐Branch Offices ☐Manufacturing Sites ☐Warehouses ☐Research Centers

☐Service Centers ☐Product Showrooms

Location of Branch Offices and Number of Representatives:

Location of Warehouses:

Location of Service Centers and Number of Service People:

Companies and Product Lines Currently Handled. Include U.S. companies.

| Company Name | Country | Product Lines/Brand Names | Since Year | Annual Sales Currency: |
|---|---|---|---|---|
|  |  |  |  |  |
|  |  |  |  |  |
|  |  |  |  |  |
|  |  |  |  |  |
|  |  |  |  |  |
|  |  |  |  |  |
|  |  |  |  |  |
|  |  |  |  |  |

Do any of the above product lines compete with our products? ☐Yes ☐No. If yes, which?

Are any of the above product lines complementary with our products? ☐ Yes ☐No. If yes, which?

Distribution Network in Our Target Market:

In what territories of the market does your company provide distribution?

What distribution channels do you use?

What customer segments do you serve?

Number of Customers:

What trade shows do you attend related to our product line?

Why do you believe you will be successful selling our product?

References:

Bank:                                    Address:

Business:                              Address:

Contact:                Title:          Fax:                    Email:

Business:                              Address:

Contact:                Title:          Fax:                    Email:

In the initial trial period, will you accept:

☐Non-exclusive agreement: ☐Yes ☐No. Sales performance objectives: ☐Yes ☐ No.

Please attach the following: ☐ Annual Report ☐Financial Information ☐Company History ☐Company's Letterhead

☐Business Card ☐Background Information on Key Personnel

Thank you for completing this profile and helping our company learn more about your company.

| Completed by: | | Title: | |
|---|---|---|---|
| Telephone: | Fax: | Email: | Date: |

Export Intermediary Profile

# 3B. Select Market Segments & Distribution  Channels

| Module/Steps | Start | End | Worksheets |
|---|---|---|---|
| SELECT MARKET SEGMENTS & DISTRIBUTION CHANNELS | | | |
| 1. Identify Information Sources | | | Segment & Channel Information Source List |
| 2. Select Market Segments | | | Market Segments Selection |
| 3. Select Distribution Channels | | | Distribution Channels Selection |
| 4. Match Market Segments by Distribution Channels | | | Match Market Segments by Distribution Channels |
| 5. Match Market Segments & Channels by Territory | | | March Market Segments & Channels by Territory |
| 6. Profile Major Distribution Customers | | | Major Distribution Customer Profiles |
| 7. Profile Preferred Distribution Channel Partners | | | Preferred Distribution Partner Profile |
| MARKET SEGMENTS & DISTRIBUTION CHANNELS SELECTED | | | |

## Objective

To select the high-priority market segments to be addressed and the most appropriate channels of distribution for each target market and ROW market.

## Discussion

Assuming your company has made a decision to use the direct export market entry method (see worksheet 3A3) for selected target and/or the ROW markets, the next task is to select the high-priority market segments to be addressed in each of these markets as well as the most appropriate channels of distribution for each segment.

For those target and/or ROW markets for which your company selected the indirect market entry method, you will typically be relying on the export intermediary to perform these tasks.

## Steps

### 1. Identify Information Sources

In the Develop EPO & Resource Network module, your company identified a number of Export Promotion Organizations and the services offered by each (see worksheet 2B3). Refer back to the EPO services for sources of information and data. Some of the sources you used to collect information for selecting the company's target markets may be a source for collecting information that can be used in analyzing the market segments and channels of distribution. For U.S. companies, the Export.Gov and USDA websites may contain studies/reports specific to your product/industry and target market.

Consider participating in trade missions to target markets and buying missions from target markets that may be sponsored by EPOs and trade associations. Use these missions to acquire intelligence about your company's target market customer segments and distribution channels. Consider purchasing market studies produced by private companies that are relevant to your product and target market.

In-market resources can be a significant source of information and data. Search out Chambers of Commerce and relevant product/industry associations and journals for insights into customer segments and channels of distribution.

Consult with staff at the relevant EPOs and trade associations as well as the staff of the foreign commercial services at your country's embassies and consulates in the target market. In the process of approaching these contacts, use an updated *Company & Product Profile* worksheet (2B2) to (re)introduce your company and to provide information that will help the contact understand your products and request for assistance.

Use the *Segments & Channels Information Source List* worksheet (3B1) to create an inventory of potential sources.

For the ROW markets (all markets except the target markets), your company's resources for researching the segments and channels may be limited. However, you may search for global product/industry segments and distribution channels that could be used for these markets.

## 2. Select Market Segments

Use the *Market Segment Selection* worksheet (3B2) to start your analysis. You will frequently find that the foreign markets will have market/customer segments similar to your domestic market. There may also be segments that are global – segments that exist and are very similar in all country markets. So, start by summarizing your company's market segments in your domestic market.

As you search for and identify market segments in the foreign market, list the various market segments and start to profile the segments – share of the total market, types of and/or major customers in the segment, categories of products purchased.

Your knowledge of the market segments will continue to develop over time, but at this point start the process of documenting the insights you are gaining about the market. Based on your research, you may be able to estimate the total size of the market for your products and thus for each market segment.

Make an initial determination of the market segments your company will plan to address and summarize the rationale for that decision.

## 3. Select Distribution Channels

The next task is to start identifying the channels of distribution in the foreign market, in relation to the market segments you have selected (3B2), using the *Distribution Channel Selection* worksheet (3B3). Again, you may find that the channels of distribution in a foreign market are similar to those in your domestic market. It is also possible the market segment for your product is served by a global distribution channel.

Start by summarizing your company's distribution channels in the domestic market.

Frequently there are multiple levels of distribution in a country (e.g., importer, regional distributor) and the levels may be different for each market segment. The terms applied to the members of the distribution channel, as well as the functions, may differ from the domestic market. Therefore, it will be important to understand these differences as you analyze the channels.

Start the task by listing the various channels, the share to the total market, the various levels in the channel, type of and/or major customers in the channel, and types of products purchased through the channel. As your understanding of the channels progresses, keep updating the worksheet. Determine the channels you anticipate using and provide your rationale for the decision.

In your analysis of the channels of distribution, you will find three approaches to distribution in a market – direct channel to the distribution customer, representative channel to the distribution customer, or direct channel to the retail customer. Now, or at some time in the near future, you will make a decision to use one approach or the other.

❑ **Direct Channel to Distribution Customer**

Use of a direct-to-customer channel means that your company will sell directly to the distribution channel's customer through one of several methods such as online, a company sales agent operating out of your domestic market, or a company sales office or subsidiary in the foreign market.

Numerous factors might influence your decision to sell directly to the customer. What, for example, are your findings regarding the customary channels customers employ to purchase product? Does your company have the resources to sell directly to customers? Does the potential total volume of sales in a channel justify selling direct? Would shipments be full containers or less-than-container loads? Are there many or only a few customers in a channel? Will training and/or after-sales service be required by the customer? Is the country a target or ROW market? What is the profit margin of your company's product? Would use of a B2B global, country, or industry marketplace platform or the company's eCommerce website be an option?

Some of the advantages of selling directly to distribution channel customers will include developing an understanding of the customers' needs and controlling the relationships with the customers.

One solution to the direct sales or representative sales decision is to use a blended approach – use a representative channel but develop a relationship with the representative whereby your company can participate in the representative's work (e.g., share in the representative's booth at a trade show).

❑ *Representative Channel to Distribution Customer*

There are certain advantages in using a representative channel of distribution. For example, a representative channel limits the investment your company is required to make in the market. Furthermore, a representative may have established relationships with the customer that will jump-start your entry into the market.

If your company decides upon a representative channel of distribution, your next decision will be to determine whether you prefer a sales agent or a distributor. There are several important differences between the typical sales agent and distributor that you will want to consider.

▪ *Sales Agent.* A sales agent (sometimes referred to as a manufacturer's representative) is an independent contractor, may be paid either a commission or a base plus a commission, and is financed by your company. The agent sells at the prices your company establishes and does not stock your products (although the product may be carried on consignment in some cases). The risk of loss, nonpayment, liability, and responsibility for service and warranty remain with you, the exporter.

▪ *Distributor.* The distributor is an independent contractor that typically purchases your product at a discount, stocks the product locally, sets the selling price, provides buyer financing, handles service and warranty needs, and assumes certain risks and liabilities. However, in using a distributor your company gives up control over pricing and marketing methods and will have no or only limited contact with the final customer. Because the distributor usually handles several product lines, you cannot be assured that your product or service will get the attention you want in the market.

The terms sales "agent" and "distributor" may be defined differently in different countries, either through common use or by law. Therefore, it is important to understand the meaning of the terms in each market.

❑ *Direct Channel to Retail Consumer*

While selling directly to the retail consumer is not typical in export markets, the availability of global and country B2C online marketplace platforms and a company eCommerce website have made cross-border direct sales to consumers an option.

### 4. *Match Market Segments by Distribution Channels*

Using the *Match Segments by Distribution Channels* worksheet (3B4) to prioritize the market segments your company will address in the foreign market, identify the channel of distribution that will be matched with each market segment, and the types of distribution channels and/or major customers in each segment.

Given that your company's understanding of the market segments and related distribution channels will be evolving over time, you will use this worksheet to maintain an updated summary of your decisions.

### 5. *Match Market Segments & Channels by Territory*

Some country markets will be dominated by national market segments and distribution channels. Other country markets may have different market segments (e.g., agriculture, manufacturing) and distribution channels in various geographic territories of the country. If the segments and channels vary by territory, use the *Match Market Segments & Channels by Territory* worksheet (3B5) to list the geographic territories and the related segments and channels.

### 6. *Profile Major Distribution Customers*

In the process of researching the market segments and channels of distribution in a given foreign market, you may identify specific major distribution customers. Capture this information on the *Major Distribution Customer Profile* worksheet (3B6). For each major user include contact information, products purchased, volume purchased, the market segment of which the user is a member, the channels used to reach the major user, and any information you find on the purchasing requirements for the user.

### 7. *Profile Preferred Distribution Channel Partners*

Before completing the segments and channels task, develop a profile of the preferred distribution partner for each market segment in each foreign market (target country and ROW). Use the *Preferred Distribution Channel Partner Profile* worksheet (3B7) for this purpose.

Some of the characteristics to be considered in profiling a potential distribution partner include: English capabilities, years in business, primary business activity, sales volume/growth, facilities/locations, sales/service personnel, complementary product lines, position in distribution channel, key customer segment served, and selling/marketing ability.

## Worksheet 3B1

## SEGMENT & CHANNEL INFORMATION SOURCE LIST

Purpose: To identify the data and information resources to be used. Directions: Select ROW or Target Market and enter the country that is to be analyzed. Identify the resource organizations, websites, and materials to be used, sources, and type of data and information to be obtained.

Company Name/Division:                                          Project:

☐ROW ☐Target Country:                                    ☐Initial ☐Update

| Organization/Materials and Source | Type Information to be Obtained | Requested | Received |
|---|---|---|---|
|  |  |  |  |
|  |  |  |  |
|  |  |  |  |
|  |  |  |  |
|  |  |  |  |
|  |  |  |  |
|  |  |  |  |
|  |  |  |  |
|  |  |  |  |
|  |  |  |  |
|  |  |  |  |
|  |  |  |  |
|  |  |  |  |
|  |  |  |  |
|  |  |  |  |
|  |  |  |  |
|  |  |  |  |
|  |  |  |  |
|  |  |  |  |

Completed by:                                          Date:

# Worksheet 3B2
## MARKET SEGMENT SELECTION

Purpose: To identify and analyze the primary market segments in the market and to select the high-potential segments. Directions: Enter the Target Market or select ROW. Summarize primary market segments in your domestic market. List market segments in foreign market. Determine market share/volume. Identify types of (or major) customers. Identify types of products purchased by each type of user. Estimate total market size at bottom of form. Select and prioritize high-potential segments and rationale for selection.

Company Name/Division:        Project:

☐ ROW ☐ Target Country:        ☐ Initial ☐ Update

Market Segments Served in Domestic Market:

| Market Segment | Mkt %/Vol | Customers in Segment | Products Purchased | Selected | Rationale |
|---|---|---|---|---|---|
|  |  |  |  |  |  |
|  |  |  |  |  |  |
|  |  |  |  |  |  |
|  |  |  |  |  |  |
|  |  |  |  |  |  |
|  |  |  |  |  |  |
|  |  |  |  |  |  |
|  |  |  |  |  |  |
|  |  |  |  |  |  |
|  |  |  |  |  |  |
|  |  |  |  |  |  |
|  |  |  |  |  |  |
|  |  |  |  |  |  |
| Total Mkt Size: |  |  |  |  |  |

Completed by:        Date:

## Worksheet 3B3

## DISTRIBUTION CHANNEL SELECTION

Purpose: To identify and analyze the primary distribution channels in the market and to select the channels with the highest potential.
Directions: Enter the Target Market or select ROW. Summarize primary distribution channels used in your domestic market. List distribution channels in foreign market. Determine market share/volume. Identify sub-levels of distribution. Identify types of (or major) customers for channel. Identify types of products purchased by each type of customer. Estimate total market size. Select and prioritize high-potential distribution channels and rationale for selection.

Company Name/Division:                                            Project:

☐ROW ☐Target Country:                                                                      ☐Initial ☐Update

Channels of Distribution in the Domestic Market:

| Channel Name | Mkt %/Vol | Channel Sub-Levels | Customers in Channel | Products Purchased | Selected | Rationale |
|---|---|---|---|---|---|---|
|  |  |  |  |  |  |  |
|  |  |  |  |  |  |  |
|  |  |  |  |  |  |  |
|  |  |  |  |  |  |  |
|  |  |  |  |  |  |  |
|  |  |  |  |  |  |  |
|  |  |  |  |  |  |  |
|  |  |  |  |  |  |  |
|  |  |  |  |  |  |  |
|  |  |  |  |  |  |  |
|  |  |  |  |  |  |  |
|  |  |  |  |  |  |  |
|  |  |  |  |  |  |  |
|  |  |  |  |  |  |  |
|  |  |  |  |  |  |  |
| Total Market Size |  |  |  |  |  |  |

Completed by:                                            Date:

# Worksheet 3B4

## MATCH MARKET SEGMENTS BY DISTRIBUTION CHANNELS

Purpose: To match selected market segments with the most appropriate selected channels of distribution. Directions: List the prioritized market segments and the estimated percentage for each segment of the total market. Match and enter the most typical first-level prioritized channel members to whom products are sold, followed by the second level and other-level channel members until you reach the customers for that market segment/channel.

Company Name/Division:

☐ROW ☐Target Country:

Project:

☐Initial ☐Update

| Prioritized Market Segment | % Mkt | Matched Prioritized Distribution Levels to Each Prioritized Market Segment | | | |
|---|---|---|---|---|---|
| | | Channel Level 1 | Channel Level 2 | Channel Levels Other | Customers |
| | | | | | |
| | | | | | |
| | | | | | |
| | | | | | |
| | | | | | |
| | | | | | |
| | | | | | |
| | | | | | |
| | | | | | |
| | | | | | |

Completed by:                                    Date:

**Worksheet 3B5**

## MATCH SEGMENTS & CHANNELS BY TERRITORY

Purpose: To identify the geographic territories by selected market segments and distribution channels. Directions: List major geographic territories in market (including national if appropriate). Identify segments in territory, size, channels used to serve segments, and relevant characteristics of segments and channels in territory. Attach map.

Company Name/Division:                                              Project:

☐ROW ☐Target Country:                                                                    ☐Initial ☐Update

| Territory | Segments & Size | Channels Used | Characteristics of Territory |
|-----------|-----------------|---------------|------------------------------|
|           |                 |               |                              |
|           |                 |               |                              |
|           |                 |               |                              |
|           |                 |               |                              |
|           |                 |               |                              |
|           |                 |               |                              |
|           |                 |               |                              |
|           |                 |               |                              |
|           |                 |               |                              |
|           |                 |               |                              |
|           |                 |               |                              |
|           |                 |               |                              |
|           |                 |               |                              |
|           |                 |               |                              |
|           |                 |               |                              |
|           |                 |               |                              |
|           |                 |               |                              |
|           |                 |               |                              |

Completed by:                                    Date:

# Worksheet 3B6

## MAJOR DISTRIBUTION CUSTOMER PROFILES

Purpose: To define the major distribution customers in the primary market segments. Directions: Identify major customers and contact information. Define primary products and volume used, segments in which user is categorized, channels through which user purchases, purchasing requirements, and other known characteristics.

Company Name/Division:        Project:

☐ ROW ☐ Target Country:        ☐ Initial ☐ Update

| Major Customer | Contact Information | Products | Vol | Segment | Channels | Requirements & Other Information |
|---|---|---|---|---|---|---|
|  |  |  |  |  |  |  |
|  |  |  |  |  |  |  |
|  |  |  |  |  |  |  |
|  |  |  |  |  |  |  |
|  |  |  |  |  |  |  |
|  |  |  |  |  |  |  |
|  |  |  |  |  |  |  |
|  |  |  |  |  |  |  |
|  |  |  |  |  |  |  |
|  |  |  |  |  |  |  |
|  |  |  |  |  |  |  |
|  |  |  |  |  |  |  |

Completed by:        Date:

**Worksheet 3B7**

**PREFERRED DISTRIBUTION CHANNEL PARTNER PROFILE**

Purpose: To define the characteristics of the preferred distribution channel partners in the market. Directions: Define type of channel member, market segments served, products promoted, and territories served. Describe characteristics of preferred distribution partner.

Company Name/Division:                                          Project:

☐ROW ☐Target Country:                                          ☐Initial ☐Update

Type of Channel Member Wanted: ☐Agent ☐Distributor ☐ Other:

Primary Market Segments to be Served by Channel Member:

Primary Products to be Promoted by Channel Member:

Primary Territories to be Served by Channel Member:

Describe Characteristics of Preferred Distribution Partner:

Completed by:                                          Date:

# 3C. Determine Product, Price & Promotion

| Module/Steps | Start | End | Worksheets |
|---|---|---|---|
| DETERMINE PRODUCT PRICE & PROMOTION | | | |
| 1. Identify Competitors in Market | | | Competitor Information Source List<br>Competitor List |
| 2. Analyze Competitor Products, Prices & Promotions | | | Market Competitor Analysis |
| 3. Develop Preliminary Product, Price & Promotion | | | Preliminary Product, Price & Promotion |
| 4. Analyze Competitive Term Options | | | Trade Term Analysis<br>Payment Term Analysis |
| 5. Analyze Competitive Unit Price Options | | | Unit Price Analysis |
| 6. Develop Introductory Product, Price & Promotion | | | Introductory Product, Price & Promotion |
| PRODUCT, PRICE & PROMOTION DETERMINED | | | |

## Objective

To determine the competitive products, prices, and promotions that will be initially offered in target and ROW markets.

## Discussion

Just as your company gathers intelligence on its competition in the domestic market, it will want to research target and ROW markets to develop an understanding of its competitors in foreign markets before establishing the company's product offerings, pricing strategies, and promotion methods.

How will the products be positioned? Can the products be competitively priced and still produce a profit? What promotional support will be required to attract good distribution partners?

## Steps

### 1. Identify Competitors in Markets

Start by identifying potential sources of competitive information on a market. Once again, consult your company's EPO and resource network (2B3) established in a previous module. If you are participating in trade or buying missions from target markets, gather intelligence from your contacts about competitors in the relevant markets. The same in-market resources (e.g., Chamber of Commerce, product/industry associations, journals, government agencies) you used to understand the distribution channels in the markets could be useful in identifying and analyzing your company's competitors in the markets.

Journal articles and advertisements, as well as company annual reports, can be very helpful in providing in-depth information on competitors. Another source of competitor information is to review the lists of companies participating in trade shows in the market. If there are domestic or in-market companies that supply *complementary* products to the foreign market, approach them for information on the market and competitors in the foreign market. Other sources of intelligence may include industry directories and market studies produced by governmental agencies and private organizations.

Use the *Competitor Information Source List* worksheet (3C1) to create an inventory of sources for identifying in-market competitors.

### 2. Analyze Competitor Product, Price & Promotion

As your company begins to gather intelligence on competitors in the market, look for both competitors located in the market and competitors from outside the market that sell into the market. Use the *Competitor List* worksheet (3C2) to record basic information on each competitor – location, contact information, website, number of employees, sales, distributors that can be identified, and its strengths and weaknesses.

For each competitor that has been identified, document the specific findings in *the Market Competitor Analysis* worksheet (3C3). Include the following information:

- Product offered in the market and estimated market share.
- Market segment served with product positioning and pricing strategy.
- Channels of distribution your competitors use in the market, as well as trade and payment terms, unit price, discounts/commission, and promotions

## 3. Develop Preliminary Product, Price & Promotions

Based on your analysis of competitors in the market, start developing your company's preliminary offering in the market using the *Preliminary Product, Price & Promotions* worksheet (3C4). This worksheet represents a first-cut version of your competitive offer in the target and ROW markets. The current task is preliminary because you will continue to research and analyze the factors that go into pricing your products before finalizing the introductory offering. Decisions made in this task will take into account the analysis that has just been completed regarding the competitors' positions in the market being considered.

> *Case Example*. The company was a start-of-the-art manufacturer of medical products and was always searching for new distribution methods that would get it closer to the customer. In one market, the company used graduate students in the country to research the market and introduce its products. The students earned commissions and class credits. The company learned a lot more about the market, its customer, and the suitability of its product than it could have ever learned from a distributor. As a result, the company was better positioned to determine the channels of distribution it wanted to use in the market.

The preliminary statement of the offering in the market should include the following information.

- *Products* – the products to be offered in the market.
- *Positioning Strategy* – how products will be differentiated from competitive products.
- *Pricing Strategy* – premium, penetration, economy, etc.
- *Channel Member* – assumed channels of distribution.
- *Order Size* – planned startup, minimum, regular.
- *Terms* – trade, payment.
- *Price* – unit price, currency.
- *Discount/Commission* – to be offered.
- *Promotions* – to be supported.
- *Services* – after-sale, warranty, etc.

The products to be offered in a specific target market are determined by the best-prospect product decisions made in a previous module (worksheet 2A2) and will be adjusted based on your current analysis of the competitors and their products in the market.

The order size may vary from your domestic startup, minimum, and regular order policies. Because the cost of shipping a small order may result in a higher unit shipping cost and, thus, an overall higher unit cost to the distribution partner, the order sizes may need to be larger to optimize the total unit cost for the distribution partner. On the other hand, if a potential buyer uses a consolidation service in your domestic market to aggregate small orders into a containerized shipment, you may be able to offer smaller order sizes to these types of buyers.

Two items on the preliminary worksheet, Terms and Price, may need to be delayed until the next tasks and worksheets in this step are completed and your company is ready to finalize the introductory product, price and promotion in worksheet 3C8.

## 4. Analyze Competitive Term Options

The two terms to be analyzed in this task are trade terms and payment terms.

❑ *Trade Terms*

Use the *Trade Term Analysis* worksheet (3C5) to analyze and select the trade terms you anticipate offering to distribution partners in a specific target market or the more general ROW market. If your product is a service, there may be no physical shipment and, thus, no need to address the trade terms issue.

The trade terms used in global trade are *Incoterms*, and these terms are revised every decade. It is important to use *Incoterms* (as opposed to domestic shipping terms) because they define in detail the responsibilities of the exporter/seller and distribution partner/buyer at every step of the export shipping process. For a full understanding of the terms, obtain a copy of the current *Incoterm* publication from the International Chamber of Commerce.

Trade terms are categorized by (a) the point of delivery and (b) the main mode of transportation. Each term defines in extensive detail the obligations of the seller and buyer under the term – export license, export clearance, carriage, insurance, delivery, transfer of risks, allocation of costs, notice, delivery documents, etc.

- *Point of Delivery*. The points of delivery are divided into four general categories that are summarily defined as follows: "E" delivery is in the seller's country (seller does not usually clear the shipment for export); "F" delivery is to the main carrier; "C" delivery is to the main carrier and seller pays shipping cost; "D" delivery is to a point in the buyer's country.

- *Main Mode of Transportation*. The main modes of transportation are generally categorized as follows: Sea by container/RoRo or non-container, Rail/Truck, Air, and Multimodal.

The simplest *Incoterm* for the company/seller, but the most cumbersome for the buyer, is Ex Works (EXW) at the company's dock (buyer arranges all transportation). Another trade term that is convenient for the exporter is Free Carrier (FCA) at a named place such as the main carrier in the exporter's country (seller arranges transportation to the carrier). A common trade term that is convenient for the buyer is Carriage and Insurance Paid To (CIP) a specific destination (typically a port in the buyer's country) where the exporter contracts for and pays the cost of carriage and insurance.

The trade term that your company will use in target markets is one that is typically convenient for the seller and the buyer such as CIP. Sometimes the buyer will be purchasing less-than-container loads (LCL) from several sellers and consolidating the combined shipments into a full container load (FCL) for export. In this case, the exporter may be able to use the EXW trade term.

In ROW markets, your company will typically use the FCA trade term in order to limit the resources devoted to arranging a shipment to the buyer's country. However, the company may want to arrange the shipment if the purchase is significant enough to warrant the company's investment of time or if the shipment can be made by an international delivery service.

❑ *Payment Terms*

Use the *Payment Term Analysis* worksheet (3C6) to determine the payment terms that your company plans to offer the buyers in specific target and ROW markets for startup and ongoing regular shipments.

The payment terms set by the company will be a factor in determining the competitiveness of its offers. In setting payment terms, two primary considerations need to be made.

- *Order Type*. Will the order be a startup or ongoing regular order? Typically, the payment terms for startup orders will be different from those for ongoing orders. It is usually reasonable for the company to request payment by credit card or cash in advance for start-up orders. As the order size increases and your experience with the buyer develops, it is reasonable that the company and buyer will move to other payment methods.

- *Risks and Costs*. How will the risks and costs be balanced between the company and buyer? When the company selects a payment method with very low collection risk (e.g. cash in advance), the buyer is usually going to find the payment method more costly and less competitive compared to payment methods that may be offered (e.g., open account) by the company's competitors in the market. As the relationship between the company and buyer develops, it is reasonable that the company and buyer will move to more competitive payment methods.

The terms of payment are a factor in determining the competitiveness of the company's offer, but they can also have an impact on the company's ability to obtain financing for export sales and other financial matters. Another factor that may influence your payment terms is country risk – the stability of the buyer's country's political and economic systems.

The following is a summary description of some of the payment term options listed on the *Payment Term Analysis* worksheet.

- *Cash in Advance*. Your buyer either pays you at the time of the order or before the product is shipped. Cash in advance is usually paid by wire transfer or online payment.

- *Letter of Credit (LC)*. The LC substitutes the credit of your buyer's bank for that of the buyer. The buyer obtains a LC from a bank in the buyer's country issued to your company and "advised" through a bank in your country. Payment under a LC will typically be at the time of shipment and your presentation of the documents specified in the LC to the advising bank with a sight draft, or within a given period, such as 90 days, with a time draft. When you submit the specified and correct documents listed in the LC to the advising bank, you have performed your responsibilities in absolute adherence to the specific terms of the LC. Otherwise, "discrepancies" will prevent you from collecting on the LC (and you will be, in effect, on open account with your buyer).

  Irrevocable LC. The LC must be an "irrevocable" LC which means that there can be no cancellation or modification of the conditions stated in the LC without mutual consent of both you and the buyer.

  Confirmed LC. Depending on the country involved, your banker may advise you to require a "confirmed" LC, whereby the LC is confirmed by the advising bank – the advising bank guarantees payment by the buyer's bank. The bank fees in the buyer's country are typically paid by your buyer and can have a significant effect on the buyer's total cost. The fees outside of the buyer's country are your cost, unless otherwise specified.

- *Collection*. The are two documentary collection methods: Documents Against Payment (D/P) and Documents Against Acceptance (D/A).

Documents Against Payment. The D/P uses a sight draft documentary collection instrument (similar to a promissory note). Your bank's services will be required to collect payment. A draft drawn on the buyer and payable to your company is prepared by you and is forwarded to your bank with the relevant document (e.g., invoice, transportation). Your bank forwards the draft and documents to its correspondent bank in your buyer's country, and the correspondent bank collects from your buyer and releases the documents to the buyer. Payment of the bank fees for the D/P services must be stipulated in your agreement with the buyer. When you use the D/P method, there are no guarantees associated with the D/P and the buyer may cancel its order prior to accepting the shipment, leaving you with your product sitting in a foreign port with no realistic way to collect.

Documents Against Acceptance. The D/A is a time draft and is processed like the D/P. However, the terms allow the buyer to receive the shipment and make payment within a given period (e.g., 90 days). The primary advantage of the D/A over Open Account terms is that you may be able to discount the D/A and receive immediate payment if the buyer's credit is strong.

- *Open Account*. The bill of lading and a commercial invoice are forwarded directly to your buyer. Depending on local business practices, open account terms can vary from net in 30 days to net in 180 days.

- Other. There are private companies (e.g. PayPal) that offer buyers and sellers payment/collection solutions.

The *Payment Term Analysis* worksheet lists an array of terms ranked from the lowest to the highest collection risk. Each term defines on whom the company relies for collection/risk and when the company will receive funds. For each payment term being selected, note the considerations your buyers may have and competitive considerations they will be evaluating. Finally, determine the payment terms for start-up and regular orders you intend to offer buyers in each of the target and ROW markets.

## 3. Analyze Competitive Unit Price Options

In this task, you will use the *Unit Price Analysis* worksheet (3C7) to develop a competitive "Unit Export Ex Works Price" for your company's product based on a set of policies and assumptions (e.g., target market, channel member, type of order, size of order). The analysis will be extremely beneficial in determining pricing in your target markets.

The step is divided into two tasks – set terms and assumptions and calculate the unit price.

❑ *Set Assumptions & Terms*

The first task in the process is to specify all the assumptions and terms you will use in preparing the competitive Unit Export Ex Works Price. Some of the information required to complete this task may be taken from the *Product, Price & Promotions: Preliminary* worksheet (2F4). Additional information for this worksheet will be based on your assumptions, preferences, and other sources.

In preparing this analysis, not every item (e.g., Import Permit #) will be required. Therefore, only the items that you will need to use in this task are noted below. The information to be specified is as follows:

- *Market Information*. State ROW or country market, market segment, channel member, and order type.
- *Product*. Use one of the products you are preliminarily considering for introduction into the selected market.

- *Sales Unit*. Define a single sales unit (e.g., case) of the selected product.
- *Order Size Export Crated*. You may assume an anticipated start-up or regular size order along with port related information.
- *Transportation Mode*. Based on the size of the shipment and destination, assume the type of carrier and load information. In order to complete the shipping costs, you may need to contact a shipping company and ask for estimates based on the above assumptions.
- *Trade Terms*. Note the Incoterms you selected in the previous worksheet.
- *Payment Terms*. Note the payment terms you selected in the previous worksheet.

❑ **Calculate Unit Price**

In calculating the unit price, you will use a "cost-plus" and "competitive" pricing method. This approach will assess the various factors in determining your price based on the assumptions and terms developed above. The steps in calculating the price are summarized below. You may want to use a spreadsheet to set up the task and perform the calculations.

- Cost-Plus Price Approach

  - ✓ *Cost-Plus Price Column*. Start with this column.
  - ✓ *Unit Domestic FOB Price*. Enter the price for one product unit. Subtract product unit costs related to your domestic market. Add product unit costs related to preparing and marketing the product in the export market.
  - ✓ *Unit Export EXW Price*. Calculate the price. Enter the total sales unit number in the order from the assumptions and terms section.
  - ✓ *Order Export EXW Price*. Calculate the price. Add the cost of any crating or marking of the shipment.
  - ✓ *Order Export Crated EXW Price*. Calculate the price. Add local carriage, forwarding and related costs.
  - ✓ *Order Export Price FCA/FAS/FOB*. Calculate the price and state the appropriate trade term (e.g., FCA). Add main carriage, insurance, and any other costs.
  - ✓ *Order Export Price CIP/CPT/CIF/DAP/DPU*. Calculate the price and state the appropriate trade term (e.g., CIP). Add import duties, VAT broker fees, on-carriage, and other related costs.
  - ✓ *Order Import Price DDP*. Calculate the price. Enter the assumed distribution partner or customer mark-up percentage.
  - ✓ *Order Import Price to Customer/Consumer*. Calculate the price. Enter the number of total sales units in the order.
  - ✓ *Unit Import Price to Customer/Consumer*. Calculate the price. This is the price of your product to the customer/consumer in the market based on the Cost-Plus Price approach.
  - ✓ *Question*. Is this price to the customer/consumer going to be competitive in the market?

- Select Competitive Price for Unit Imported Price to Customer/Consumer

  - ✓ *Question*. Based on the company's previous analysis (worksheets 3C2 and 3C3), is the Cost-Plus Price approach going to generate a competitive price to the customers/consumers in the market?
  - ✓ *Select Competitive Price for Unit Import Price to Customer/Consumer*. Select the unit price at which you believe your product should be sold in order to be

> *Case Example. A company with no export experience received an inquiry from a distributor in Europe. The company quoted a price based on its domestic price plus costs and started making regular shipments to the distributor. After three years, the company visited the distributor and discovered that the distributor was selling the product at a 250% mark-up. Had the company competitively priced its product to the market, it could have participated in the large profit margin.*

competitive to customers/consumers in the market. Enter that competitive price in this line in the

Cost-Plus column and the Competitive Price column. The price may be below, at, or higher than the calculated *Unit Import Price to Customer/Consumer*.

- Competitive Price Approach

  - ✓ *Competitive Price Column*. Start at the bottom of the column.
  - ✓ *Select Competitive Price for Unit Import Price to Customer/Consumer*. Enter the competitive price you selected in the above task.
  - ✓ *Recalculate*. Work back up the Competitive Price column.
  - ✓ *Unit Export EXW Price*. This is the unit price your company would have to offer a distribution partner in order to be competitive in the market based on the analysis and assumptions you have made up to this point.

- Finalize Unit Export EXW Price

  - ✓ *Question*. Is the *Unit Export EXW Price* calculated in the Competitive Price column above, below, or similar to the price in the Cost-Plus column?
  - ✓ *Considerations*. If the competitive price is higher than the cost-plus price, your company has the potential to sell the product at a price above the price charged to buyers in your domestic market. This would allow you to increase your profit margin on this product. However, if the competitive price is lower than your price to buyers in your domestic market, you may have a problem in competing in the foreign market and maintaining your existing profit margin for the product. Can you find a way to reduce costs? Can you position your product to make it competitive even at a higher price? Maybe you cannot be competitive in the market with this product at this time. Do you need more in-depth knowledge of the market, competitors, distribution channels, and end buyers before you can make a final decision on products, prices, and promotions for the market? Would an increase in the number of units produced lower your overall unit production costs and, thus, justify selling your product at a lower unit price?
  - ✓ *Finalize Unit Export EXW Price*. At this point, you may be in a position to finalize your market entry price or you may need to continue using a preliminary price in your next tasks. State your rationale for setting the price.

The pricing of your product in a foreign market is a critical decision – you can end up increasing or decreasing your profit margin for a product. A common mistake made by many exporters is to use only a Cost Plus pricing method without accounting for the price of the product in the target market. This can, in many cases, result in underpricing the product to the company's distribution partner, thus giving up profit that will then be captured by the distribution partner. Once this profit is given to the distribution partner, it is very difficult to renegotiate the price with them.

## 4. Develop Final Introductory Product, Price & Promotion

After completing the *Unit Price Analysis* worksheet, your company may be in a position to finalize the *Introductory Product, Price &* Promotion worksheet (3C8). This worksheet will be the *starting point* for your negotiations with potential distribution partners.

As the company's knowledge of target and ROW markets increases, this worksheet will be continuously updated to keep it current.

**Worksheet 3C1**

**COMPETITOR INFORMATION SOURCE LIST**

Purpose: To identify the data and information resources to be used. Directions: Identify the resource organizations and materials to be used, sources, and type of data and information to be obtained. Note when requested and received.

Company Name/Division:                                    Project:

☐ROW ☐Target Country:                                                            ☐Initial ☐Update

| Organization & Materials/Source | Type of Information to be Obtained | Requested | Received |
|---|---|---|---|
| | | | |
| | | | |
| | | | |
| | | | |
| | | | |
| | | | |
| | | | |
| | | | |
| | | | |
| | | | |
| | | | |
| | | | |
| | | | |
| | | | |
| | | | |

Completed by:                                    Date:

# Worksheet 3C2

## COMPETITOR LIST

Purpose: To identify competitors in the market. Directions: List identified competitors and other information obtained on each competitor.

Company Name/Division:                                              Project:

☐ROW ☐Target Country:                                   ☐Initial ☐Update

| Company | Location | Contact & Info | Website | #Empl | Sales | Distributors | Strengths/Weaknesses |
|---------|----------|----------------|---------|-------|-------|--------------|----------------------|
|         |          |                |         |       |       |              |                      |
|         |          |                |         |       |       |              |                      |
|         |          |                |         |       |       |              |                      |
|         |          |                |         |       |       |              |                      |
|         |          |                |         |       |       |              |                      |
|         |          |                |         |       |       |              |                      |
|         |          |                |         |       |       |              |                      |
|         |          |                |         |       |       |              |                      |
|         |          |                |         |       |       |              |                      |
|         |          |                |         |       |       |              |                      |
|         |          |                |         |       |       |              |                      |
|         |          |                |         |       |       |              |                      |
|         |          |                |         |       |       |              |                      |
|         |          |                |         |       |       |              |                      |
|         |          |                |         |       |       |              |                      |
|         |          |                |         |       |       |              |                      |
|         |          |                |         |       |       |              |                      |
|         |          |                |         |       |       |              |                      |

Completed by:                                              Date:

# Worksheet 3C3

## MARKET COMPETITOR ANALYSIS

Purpose: To analyze the competition in the market. Directions: Indicate major products sold in market and estimated market share by segments serviced (product position, price, pricing strategy) and channels of distribution (trade and payment terms, unit price, discounts, and promotions used).

Company Name/Division:                                    Project:

☐ROW ☐Target Country:                                    ☐Initial ☐Update

| Competitor | Products in Market | | Market Segments Served | | | Channels of Distribution Used | | | | |
|---|---|---|---|---|---|---|---|---|---|---|
| | Product | Mkt %/ Vol | Segments | Product Position | Price / Strategy | Member Type | Trade & Pay Terms | Unit Price | Discount/ Commission | Promotions Used |
| | | | | | | | | | | |
| | | | | | | | | | | |
| | | | | | | | | | | |
| | | | | | | | | | | |
| | | | | | | | | | | |
| | | | | | | | | | | |
| | | | | | | | | | | |
| | | | | | | | | | | |
| | | | | | | | | | | |
| | | | | | | | | | | |
| | | | | | | | | | | |

Completed by:                                    Date:

# Worksheet 3C4

## PRELIMINARY PRODUCT, PRICE & PROMOTIONS

Purpose: To preliminarily determine the products to be introduced into the market, the pricing strategy, and the promotions to be used. Directions: For each product category to be sold in the market, develop policies for positioning, pricing, and promotion.

Company Name/Division:                                    Project:

☐ROW ☐Target Country:                                    ☐Initial ☐Update

| Product | Product Positioning | Price Strategy | Channel Members | Order Size | Trade & Pay Terms | Unit Price & Currency | Discounts/ Commissions | Promotions To Be Used | Service Etc. |
|---|---|---|---|---|---|---|---|---|---|
| | | | | | | | | | |
| | | | | | | | | | |
| | | | | | | | | | |
| | | | | | | | | | |
| | | | | | | | | | |
| | | | | | | | | | |
| | | | | | | | | | |
| | | | | | | | | | |

Completed by:                                    Date:

## Worksheet 3C5

## TRADE TERM ANALYSIS

Purpose: To select the preferred trade terms for the market. Directions: Select and circle the transportation mode in the top row. Select and circle the point of delivery to the customer in the left column. Use the matrix to identify the appropriate trade terms; if more than one trade term may be used, select the desired term. Reference: current Incoterms.

Company Name/Division:                                  Project:

☐ROW ☐Target Country:                                                              ☐Initial ☐Update

| Point of Delivery | Main Mode of Transportation | | | | |
| --- | --- | --- | --- | --- | --- |
| | Sea | | Rail/Truck | Air | Multimodal |
| | Container/RoRo | Non-Container | | | |
| "E" Destinations: Seller delivers shipment to buyer at seller's premises or another named place in seller's country. Seller does not need to clear the goods for export. Risk transfers there. | EXW | EXW | EXW | EXW | EXW |
| "F" Destinations: Seller delivers shipment to carrier or other person appointed by buyer in seller's country. Risk transfers there. | FCA | FCA FAS FOB | FCA | FCA | FCA |
| "C" Destinations: Seller delivers shipment to carrier or another person selected by seller and seller arranges and pays shipping costs to the named place of destination. Risk transfers at delivery to carrier or person selected. | CPT CIP | CPT CIP CFR CIF | CPT CIP | CPT CIP | CPT CIP |
| "D" Destinations: Seller delivers shipment to named destination. Risk transfers there. | DAP DPU DDP | DAP DPU DDP | DAP DPU DDP | DAP DPU DDP | DAP DPU DDP |

EXW: Ex Works. FCA: Free Carrier. FAS: Free Alongside Ship. FOB: Free On Board. CIP: Carriage and Insurance Paid To. CPT: Carriage Paid To. CIF: Cost, Insurance and Freight. CFR: Cost and Freight. DAP: Delivery at Place. DPU: Delivered at Place Unloaded. DDP: Delivered Duty Paid. Delivered Duty Paid. *Note: Refer to latest version of Incoterms for detailed definition of each term.*

What transportation modes will be used for: Start-Up Orders: _____ ;Regular Orders: _____

Rationale:

What points of delivery will be selected for: Start-Up Orders: _____ ;Regular Orders: _____

Rationale:

What specific Incoterms trade terms will be selected for: Start-Up Orders: _____ ;Regular Orders: _____

Rationale:

Completed by:                                                          Date:

# Worksheet 3C6

## PAYMENT TERM ANALYSIS

Purpose: To establish the preferred payment terms. Directions: Note the buyer and competitive considerations. Rate the appropriateness of the term on a scale of 0 to10. Select the most appropriate term and state the terms in detail.

Company Name/Division:  Project:
☐ROW ☐Target Country:  ☐Initial ☐Update

| Payment Terms | Company Considerations | | Buyer Considerations | Competitive Considerations | Rating |
|---|---|---|---|---|---|
| | Collection Risk | Time of Receipt Of Funds | | | |
| Credit Card | Rely on credit of credit card company | After deposit, and before shipment. | | | |
| Cash in Advance | None | Before shipment | | | |
| Confirmed Letter of Credit Sight Draft (D/P) | Rely on credit of domestic paying bank | After shipment, and upon presentation/acceptance of documents/draft | | | |
| Confirmed Letter of Credit Time Draft (D/A) | Rely on credit of domestic paying bank | After shipment, after presentation/ Acceptance of documents/draft, and upon maturity of draft | | | |
| | | After shipment, and after presentation/acceptance of documents/draft if draft is discountable | | | |
| Letter of Credit Sight Draft(D/P) | Rely on credit of Foreign paying bank | After shipment, and upon presentation/acceptance of documents/draft | | | |
| Letter of Credit Time Draft (D/A) | Rely on credit of foreign paying bank | After shipment, after presentation/ acceptance of documents/draft, and upon maturity of draft | | | |
| | | After shipment, and after presentation/ acceptance of documents/draft if draft Is discountable | | | |
| Collection Sight Draft (D/P) | Rely on credit of buyer | After shipment, and upon presentation/ acceptance of documents/draft to buyer | | | |
| Collection Time Draft (D/A) | Rely on credit of buyer | After shipment, after presentation/ acceptance of documents/draft to buyer, And upon maturity of draft | | | |
| | | After shipment, and after presentation/ acceptance of documents/draft to buyer If draft is discountable | | | |
| Open Account With Credit Insurance | Rely primarily on credit of buyer. Rely secondarily on insurer. | After shipment, and upon negotiated terms,(e.g.,180 days) | | | |
| Open Account | Rely on credit of buyer | After shipment, and upon negotiated terms(e.g. net 45 days) | | | |
| Other: | | | | | |

Payment terms for Start-up Orders(state in detail):
  Rationale:
Payment terms for Regular Orders (state in detail):
  Rationale:

Completed by:  Date:

# Worksheet 3C7
## UNIT PRICE ANALYSIS

Purpose: To determine a cost-plus and competitive Unit Export EXW price. Directions: State the assumptions and terms regarding the product, order, and other information. Determine the Cost-Plus Price by starting with your current Unit Domestic FOB Price and working down the column. Determine the Competitive Price to a customer/consumer. Recalculate the Unit Export EXW Price in the Competitive Price column by working back up the column. State final price.

Customer Name/Division     Project:     Sub-Project:     ☐Initial ☐ Update

☐ROW ☐Target Country:     Market Segment:     Channel Member:     ☐Start-Up ☐Regular

Product:     HS Number:

    Measurement Units Used: ☐ US ton ☐ Metric ton ☐ Lb. ☐Kg ☐Foot ☐ Meter ☐Other:

Sales Unit. Define Single Sales Unit:     Net Weight:     Gross Weight:

    Dimensions:

    Cube:

    Dimensional Weight (LxWxH / if inches 139 for Lb or if cm 5000 for Kg):     (Check with carrier for factors)

    Country of Origin:     ☐New ☐Used     Import Permit#:     , Expires:

Order Export Crated.    Total # Sales Units:

    Point of Origin:     Deliver to Main Carrier at:     Destination:

    Port of Loading:     Port of Unloading:

    Total Net Weight:     Total Gross Weight:

    Total Cube:

    Total Dimensional Weight:     Type Crating:

    Shipping Unit Based on: ☐Weight ☐ Dimensions ☐Dimensional Weight

Transportation Mode: ☐Ocean Containerized ☐Ocean Non-Containerized ☐Air ☐Multimodal ☐Other:

    Load: ☐FCL ☐LCL ☐ BBLK ☐ Deck ☐Under Deck ☐ Ventilation ☐ Refrigerate ☐ Other:

    Container Internal Dimensions:     Cube:

    Delivery Time Constraints:     Notes:

    Main Carrier:     Freight Rate:     Surcharges:     Other Charges:

    Cost Per Freight Unit:     Total # Freight Units:     Special Services:

Trade Terms: ☐EXW ☐FCA ☐CIP ☐CPT ☐DDP ☐Other:     at

Payment Terms: ☐Cash Advance ☐LC ☐DP ☐DA at ____days, ☐Open Account ☐Other:

    Currency:     Exchange Rate:     Price Valid Thru:

| Pricing Factors | Cost-Plus Price Per | | Competitive Price Per | |
| --- | --- | --- | --- | --- |
| | Unit | Order | Unit | Order |
| **Unit Domestic FOB Price @**_____ | _____ | | | |
|     Domestic Marketing/Warranty/Service/Drawback | -_____ | | | |
|     Other Domestic Subsidies/Savings | -_____ | | | |
|     Export Product Modification/Packaging/Warranty/Service Costs | +_____ | | | |
|     Export Marketing/Sales Agent Costs | +_____ | | | |
|     Export Financing Costs | +_____ | | | |
|     Other Export Product Costs | +_____ | | | |
| **Unit Export EX WORKS Price @** _____ | =_____ | | =_____ | |
|     Total # Sales Units Ordered | x_____ | | /_____ | |
| **Order Export EX WORKS Price @** _____ | | =_____ | | =_____ |

Unit Price Analysis          Continued          Page 1 of 2

| Pricing Factors (continued) | Cost-Plus Price Per | | Competitive Price Per | |
|---|---|---|---|---|
| | Unit | Order | Unit | Order |
| **Order Export EX WORKS Price @ _____** (Continued) | =_____ | | =_____ | |
|    Export Crating/Marking Costs | +_____ | | -_____ | |
| **Order Export Crated EX WORKS Price @ _____** | =_____ | | =_____ | |
|    Local Cartage | +_____ | | -_____ | |
|    Pre-Carriage Inland Freight by: _____ to _____ | +_____ | | -_____ | |
|    Unloading Costs at: _____ | +_____ | | -_____ | |
|    Terminal/Pier Delivery Costs | +_____ | | -_____ | |
|    Demurrage Costs | +_____ | | -_____ | |
|    Special Ship Loading Costs | +_____ | | -_____ | |
|    Consular Fees | +_____ | | -_____ | |
|    Certificate Fees | +_____ | | -_____ | |
|    Freight Forwarder Fees Include: ☐Courier ☐Banking Documents | +_____ | | -_____ | |
|    Credit Insurance/LC/Other Costs: | +_____ | | -_____ | |
| **Order Export Price:** ☐FCA ☐FAS ☐FOB @ _____ | =_____ | | =_____ | |
|    Main Carriage Freight Costs & Surcharges to: _____ | +_____ | | -_____ | |
|    Transport Insurance Costs @ 110% of CIP/CIF. Type:_____ | +_____ | | -_____ | |
|    Other Costs: _____ | +_____ | | -_____ | |
| **Order Export Price:** ☐CIP ☐CPT ☐CIF ☐DAP ☐DPU @ _____ | =_____ | | =_____ | |
|    Import Duties and Charges @ _____ | +_____ | | -_____ | |
|    Taxes/VAT @ _____ | +_____ | | -_____ | |
|    Custom House Broker Fees | +_____ | | -_____ | |
|    On-Carriage Foreign Inland Freight Costs | +_____ | | -_____ | |
|    Foreign Banking Fees | +_____ | | -_____ | |
|    Other Costs: _____ | +_____ | | | |
| **Order Import Price:** ☐DDP @ _____ | =_____ | | =_____ | |
|    Distributor/Other/Customer Mark Up @ (\_\_\_% + 100%) | x_____ | | /_____ | |
| **Order Import Price to Customer/Consumer** | =_____ | | =_____ | |
|    Total # Sales Units Ordered | /_____ | | x_____ | |
| **Unit Import Price to Customer/Consumer** | =_____ | | | |
| | _____ | | _____ | |
| **Select Competitive Price for Unit Import Price to Customer/Consumer:** | | | | |

**Rationale for setting Select Competitive Price for Import Price to Customer/Consumer:**

**Finalize Unit Export EXW Price:**           **Rationale:**

| Completed by: | Date: |
|---|---|

Unit Price Analysis            Page 2 of 2

# Worksheet 3C8

## INTRODUCTORY PRODUCT, PRICE & PROMOTIONS

Purpose: To determine the introductory products to be introduced into the market, the pricing strategy, and the promotions to be used.
Directions: For each product category to be sold in the market, develop policies for positioning, pricing, and promotion.

Company Name/Division:                                    Project:

☐ROW ☐Target Country:                                                          ☐Initial ☐Update

| Product | Product Position | Price Strategy | Channel Members | Minimum Order Size | Trade & Pay Terms | Unit Price & Currency | Discounts/ Commissions | Promotions To Be Used | Service Etc. |
|---|---|---|---|---|---|---|---|---|---|
| | | | | | | | | | |
| | | | | | | | | | |
| | | | | | | | | | |
| | | | | | | | | | |
| | | | | | | | | | |
| | | | | | | | | | |
| | | | | | | | | | |
| | | | | | | | | | |

Completed by:                                                  Date:

# 3D. Develop Target Market Profiles

| Module/Steps | Start | End | Worksheets |
|---|---|---|---|
| DEVELOP TARGET MARKET PROFILES | | | |
| 1. Summarize Market Indicator Findings | | | Target Market Profile |
| 2. Summarize Market Findings | | | |
| 3. Summarize Competitive Product, Price & Promotion Findings | | | |
| TARGET MARKET PROFILES DEVELOPED | | | |

## Objective

To develop profiles of the target markets.

## Discussion

A profile of each target market should be evolving based on the modules that have been completed. The current task is to summarize the significant findings for each target market. The profile should be continuously updated as the company's increasing knowledge of a target market evolves.

## Steps

Use the *Target Market Profile* worksheet (3D1) to summarize the findings on each target market.

1. **Summarize Market Indicator Findings**

   The Target High-Potential Markets task used a series of market selection indicators to assist in identifying the company's high-potential target markets. Summarize the important indicators that were used to determine a specific target market.

2. **Summarize Market Findings**

   Briefly summarize the findings related to each target market including market entry method, primary market segments, primary channels of distribution, and territories in the market.

3. **Summarize Competitive Product, Price & Promotion Findings**

   Briefly summarize the primary competitors the company will face in the market and the findings with regard to products, price, and promotion in the target market.

**Worksheet 3D1**

## TARGET MARKET PROFILE

Purpose: To develop a profile of the target markets. Directions: Summarize important findings to date.

Company Name/Division:

Target Country:

Project:

☐Initial ☐Update

Population:      GDP:      GDP/Capita:      Currency:      Exchange Rate:

**Market Indicator Summary Findings:**

**Market Entry Method Selected:**

**Market Segment Summary Findings:**

**Channels of Distribution Summary Findings:**

**Territories Summary Findings:**

**Competitor Summary Findings:**

**Competitive Product, Price & Promotion Summary Findings:**

**General Market Information:**

Completed by:      Date:

# 3E. Finalize Export Market Plans

| Module/Steps | Start | End | Worksheets |
|---|---|---|---|
| FINALIZE EXPORT MARKET PLANS | | | |
| 1. Define Current Activities, Market Information & Products | | | Market Export Plan |
| 2. Define Market Entry Method, Segments, Channels & Positioning | | | |
| 3. Establish Objectives, Implementation Activities & Resources | | | |
| 4. Develop Export Budget | | | Market Export Budget |
| EXPORT MARKET PLANS FINALIZED | | | |

## Objective

To finalize the export market plans for the company's target markets and the ROW market.

## Discussion

An export market plan is prepared for each target market and the ROW market. A summary global export market plan may be prepared that incorporates the individual target and ROW plans. The elements in the plan may be expanded to include other information that your company uses in preparing its plans.

During the steps that have led up to this point in the FasTrack Process, you will have assembled many facts related to your best-prospect products, highest-potential markets, competition, and many other factors. You will have also made a series of assumptions to fill in the gaps between the facts you have gathered. Assumptions are a mix of facts, judgments, and assumed states that you have sifted out of the planning module and upon which you have based your planning decisions.

As your research and planning become more sophisticated in the future, you will obtain information that can be measured against the assumptions made during this planning process. Obviously, the more acquainted you become with the worldwide and specific markets, the more accurate your assumptions will be.

Additional resources over and above the company's normal budget may have to be allocated to your company's market expansion plan. These costs may range from as little as a few thousand dollars into the tens of thousands of dollars, depending on the number of prioritized target markets your company has selected and the types of implementation activities you include in your export marketing plans. One major cost factor that you may include in your export market plan is a visit to the foreign markets and/or participation in a foreign trade show. While it is usually advisable to include a visit to the target markets in your budget, the significant cost of a trip has to be weighed against several factors, including the potential sales volume your company might expect from the market. Ideally, there would be resources for one visit to each target market.

In addition to financial resources, people and time must also be allocated in order to implement the market expansion program. Staff will have to be assigned to visit with EPOs and export service organizations, prepare promotion and response materials, respond to foreign buyer inquiries, learn how to prepare export documentation forms, etc. Someone will also have to assume the responsibility for leading and/or coordinating the export program.

> *Case Example.* The company's initial export "plan" consisted of a long-term sales goal and an outline of the company's marketing strategies and policies covering such things as pricing, distribution, product return, currencies of payment, promotion, and protection of intellectual property. The outline represented enough of a plan to successfully start up the export program and offered enough flexibility for adapting to unique market conditions in different target markets.

> *Case Example.* The company was a national non-profit educational and service organization. It decided to change its mission and name in order to expand its area of concern to include the world. In the early stages of its expansion, the company assigned one person to deal with international program activities. After several years, that person left the organization, and management found that it was without any international expertise. In fact, the company had never "internationalized" its operations -- it merely had a program that included an international component. As a result of this experience, management made a strategic decision that in the future it would use a project management approach to direct its international operations. The result was that every manager and department of the organization began to think "global" and was prepared to take advantage of opportunities to improve the lives of clients no matter where they may be in the world.

Many organizations believe that they have been more successful in exporting in the long run because they used a companywide approach rather than assigning a single person to be the export "expert." Organizations using the companywide approach have involved top management and unit managers in the export process. As a result, they have made major strides toward globalizing their company as part of the export expansion process, thereby better positioning it to deal with the long-term changes that will have to be made when the company develops a more significant commitment to global markets.

## Steps

Use the *Market Export Plan* worksheet (3E1) and *Market Export Budget* (3E2) worksheets to develop the company's plans and budget.

### 1. Define Current Activities, Market Information & Product

If the company has any current activities in the market, summarize those activities (e.g., distribution, sales) in the market. Summarize the significant findings for the market (e.g., rationale for selection of a target market, estimated market size, segment, channels, and competition). Reference worksheets 2C8, 3B2, 3C3 and 3D1.

### 2. Define Market Entry Method, Segments, Channels & Positioning

Briefly note the market entry method to be used in the market, the primary market segments to be addressed, and the channels of distribution to be used for each market segment. State the introductory product positioning, price and price positioning, expected trade terms, planned start up and regular payment terms to be offered, in-market promotions to be used, in-market services to be provided, and other planned offerings. Reference worksheets 3A3, 3B2, 3B3, 3B4, 3B5, 3C8, and 3D1.

### 3. Establish Objectives, implementation Activities & Resources

State the planned objectives for the market for the current period (e.g., year) and a five-year or similar period objective. Detail the implementation activities to be undertaken in the market (e.g., visits to the market, shows in the market, distributor search); at this point, the specific nature of the activities may not be known (e.g., which trade show). Create a timetable for implementing the activities. Identify the company resources (e.g., personnel, budget) that will be allocated to the market, and specify the non-company resources (e.g., export promotion organizations, export service organizations) that will be used to extend the limited resources of the company.

### 4. Develop Export Budget

Summarize the company's projected sales and expenses for each target market and the ROW market. List the market segments to be addressed, primary products to be promoted, and the estimated size of the market.

## Worksheet 3E1

## MARKET EXPORT PLAN

Purpose: To develop the export plan for Target or ROW market. Directions: Summarize current activities, findings and assumptions, and opportunities and threats. Identify market entry method. Establish objectives, strategies, implementation activities, and financial projections.

Company Name/Division:                                        Project:

☐ROW ☐Target Country:                        Period:            to                        ☐Initial ☐Update

**Current Activities in Market (distribution, sales):**

**Summary Market Information (rationale for selection, market size, segments, channels, competition):**

**Products to be Promoted:**

**Market Entry Method:**

**Market Segments and Distribution Channel Strategies:**

**Product Positioning, Pricing, Terms, Promotion and Service Strategies/Policies:**

**Objectives (current year):**

**Objectives (next five years):**

**Implementation Activities & Timetable:**

**Company Resources to be Used (budget, staff):**

**Non-Company Resources to be Used:**

**Attachments:**

Completed by:                                        Date:

# Worksheet 3E2

## MARKET EXPORT BUDGET

Purpose: To project annual export sales and expenses for each market by priority market segment. Directions: List priority segments, primary products to be offered to that segment, estimated total market size, and projected sales and expenses.

Company Name/Division:　　　　　　　　　　　　Project:

☐ROW ☐Target Country:　　　Period:　　　to　　　　　　　　　　　　☐Initial ☐Update

| Market Segments | Primary Products | Market Size | Sales | | | Expense Amount | Comments |
|---|---|---|---|---|---|---|---|
| | | | Mkt % | Amount | Volume | | |
| | | | | | | | |
| | | | | | | | |
| | | | | | | | |
| | | | | | | | |
| | | | | | | | |
| | | | | | | | |
| | | | | | | | |
| | | | | | | | |
| | | | | | | | |
| | | | | | | | |
| | | | | | | | |
| | | | | | | | |

Completed by:　　　　　　　　　　　　　　Date:

# 3F. Evaluate Export Market Expansion Plan Results

| Module/Steps | Start | End | Worksheets |
|---|---|---|---|
| **EVALUATE EXPORT MARKET EXPANSION PLAN RESULTS** <br><br> 1. Evaluate Current and Five-Year Objectives <br><br> 2. Evaluate Market Entry Methods & Positioning <br><br> 3. Evaluate Implementation Activities <br><br> **EXPORT MARKET EXPANDION PLAN RESULTS EVALUATED** | | | Evaluate Export Market Plan Results |

## Objective

To evaluate the degree to which the targeted export market plan results were achieved.

## Discussion

The evaluation task will assist the company in periodically examining the target export market plans and in assessing the ongoing progress toward achieving the targeted export plan objectives.

Involving your export team in the evaluation task will improve the input into the evaluations process and lead to a more accurate pinpointing of the areas of strength, weakness, and needed action steps. Finally, their involvement will also increase each team member's commitment to the achievement of increased results from, and the effectiveness of, the adjustments you make to your program.

## Steps

Use the *Evaluate Export Market Expansion Plan Results* worksheet (3F1) to complete the evaluation.

### 1. *Evaluate Current & Five-Year Objectives*

Assess the current year and five-year objectives and progress toward achieving those objectives. Identify needed adjustments in the next planning cycle.

### 2. *Evaluate Market Entry Methods & Positioning*

Assess the current year decisions with regard to the market entry methods selected, the product positioning and pricing, the trade and payment terms used, and the promotions and services used in the market. Identify needed adjustments in the next planning cycle.

### 3. *Evaluate Implementation Activities*

Assess the activities used to achieve the objectives in the market. Identify needed adjustments in the next planning cycle.

**Worksheet 3F1**

# EVALUATE EXPORT MARKET PLAN RESULTS

Purpose: To evaluate the degree to which the targeted export market plan results were achieved. Directions: This evaluation should be conducted at least annually and lead to adjustments in the next round of planning in order to align the decisions made and tasks implemented with current conditions.

| Company Name/Division: | Project: | | |
|---|---|---|---|
| ☐ROW ☐Target Country: | Period: | to: | ☐Initial ☐Update |

| Objective and Progress | %Achieved |
|---|---|

**Current Year Objectives:**

List the three most significant objectives (worksheet 3E1), degree to which achieved, and needed adjustments.

1 To …
What specific progress has been made? What adjustments are needed? _____ %

2 To …
What specific progress has been made? What adjustments are needed? _____ %

3 To …
What specific progress has been made? What adjustments are needed? _____ %

**Five-Year Objectives:**          to

List the three most significant objectives (worksheet 3E1), degree to which achieved, and needed adjustments.

1 To…
What specific progress has been made? What adjustments are needed? _____ %

2 To …
What specific progress has been made? What adjustments are needed? _____ %

3 To …
What specific progress has been made? What adjustments are needed? _____ %

**Market Entry Method**. Needed adjustments.

**Product Positioning, Pricing, Terms, Promotions, Services**. Needed adjustments.

**Implementation Activities**. Needed adjustments.

| Completed by: | Date: |
|---|---|

# APPENDICES

## Feedback

We need your feedback for the next edition.

Go to **https://www.surveymonkey.com/r/WPN29RT** and give us your review. Thank you.

## FasTrack Globalizer Cloud-Based Web Solution

For information about our FasTrack Globalizer cloud-based web export expansion solution, please contact us at info@FasTrackGlobalizer.com or visit www.FasTrackGlobalizer.com.

## Links

Please note that links change from time to time. If a link does not work, use the title to search for an updated link. Note that Export.gov is transitioning to Trade.gov.

Canada Agriculture and Agri-Food
   http://www.agr.gc.ca/eng/industry-markets-and-trade/agri-food-trade-services-for-exporters/?id=1432136045585
Canada Border Services Agency
   https://www.cbsa-asfc.gc.ca/comm-eng.html
Canada. Global Affairs Canada, Export Controls Division
   https://www.international.gc.ca/controls-controles/index.aspx?lang=eng
Canada Statistics, Canadian Export Classification (Harmonized System Code)
   https://www150.statcan.gc.ca/n1/pub/65-209-x/65-209-x2018000-eng.htm
Canada Trade Agreements
   https://www.canada.ca/en/services/business/trade/negotiations-agreements.html
Canada Trade Commissioner Service
   https://canadabusiness.ca/growing/exporting-and-importing/exporting/starting-to-export/organizations-that-can-help-you-export/
Canada Trade Data Online
   http://www.ic.gc.ca/eic/site/tdo-dcd.nsf/eng/Home
Customs Info
   http://export.customsinfo.com/Default.aspx
Euromonitor
   https://www.euromonitor.com/usa
Export.Gov
   www.export.gov
Export.Gov, Country Commercial Guides
   https://www.export.gov/ccg
Export.Gov, Market Intelligence
   https://beta.trade.gov/fta/tariff-rates-search

Export.Gov, Trade Data & Analysis
    https://www.export.gov/Trade-Data-and-Analysis
Export-U, Exporter's Database
    www.export-u.com
Global Trade Information Service
    www.gtis.com
International Chamber of Commerce, Publications, Incoterms
    https://2go.iccwbo.org/incoterms-2020-eng-config+book_version-Book/
International Trade Center
    http://www.intracen.org/
Import Genius
    https://www.importgenius.com/
Kompass International
    www.kompass.com
Minnesota District Export Council,
    www.exportassistance.com
Organization for Economic Co-operation and Development (OECD)
    http://www.oecd.org/about/
Port Import Export Reporting System (PIERS)
    www.ihsmarkit.com/products/piers.html
The World Bank, Ease of Doing Business Index
    http://www.doingbusiness.org/en/rankings
Trade.Gov
    www.trade.gov
Trade.Gov, Top Markets
    https://www.trade.gov/topmarkets/
United Nations, UN Comtrade
    http://comtrade.un.org/db/dqBasicQuery.aspx
United Nations, UN Trade Statistics, Harmonized Community Descriptions and Coding System (HS.
    https://unstats.un.org/unsd/tradekb/Knowledgebase/50018/Harmonized-Commodity-Description-and-Coding-Systems-HS?Keywords=HS
US Census Bureau, Foreign Trade, Schedule B
    https://www.census.gov/foreign-trade/schedules/b/index.html
US Census Bureau, NAICS Codes
    www.census.gov/eos/www/naics/
US Census Bureau, USA Trade Online
    https://usatrade.census.gov/
US Central Intelligence Agency, The World Factbook
    https://www.cia.gov/library/publications/the-world-factbook/
US Department of Agriculture, Foreign Agricultural Service
    https://www.fas.usda.gov/
US Department of Commerce, Bureau of Industry and Security
    https://www.bis.doc.gov/index.php/regulations/commerce-control-list-ccl
US Department of Commerce, Free Trade Agreement Tool
    https://beta.trade.gov/fta
US Department of Commerce, Trade & Policy Analysis
    https://tpis1.trade.gov/cgi-bin/wtpis/prod/tpis.cgi
US Department of Commerce, US and Foreign Commercial Service
    https://www.export.gov/article?id=U-S-and-Foreign-Commercial-Service-USFCS

US Department of State, United States Munitions List (USML)
  https://www.ecfr.gov/cgi-bin/text-idx?SID=86008bdffd1fb2e79cc5df41a180750a&node=22:1.0.1.13.58&rgn=div5
US Export Import Bank
  www.exim.gov
US Small Business Administration
  www.sba.gov/about-offices-content/1/2889
World Bank Group, World Integrated Trade Solutions
  https://wits.worldbank.org/CountryProfile/en/CAN

Lightning Source UK Ltd.
Milton Keynes UK
UKHW030705271220
375899UK00013B/1538